C000187080

WELCOME

— to —

PARENTHOOD

summersdale

WELCOME TO PARENTHOOD

Text by Isabelle Loynes

An Hachette UK Company
www.hachette.co.uk

Summersdale Publishers Ltd
Part of Octopus Publishing Group Limited
Carmelite House
50 Victoria Embankment
LONDON
EC4Y 0DZ
UK

www.summersdale.com

Printed and bound in China

ISBN: 978-1-80007-159-9

Substantial discounts on bulk quantities of Summersdale books are available to corporations, professional associations and other organizations. For details contact general enquiries: telephone: +44 (0) 1243 771107 or email: enquiries@summersdale.com.

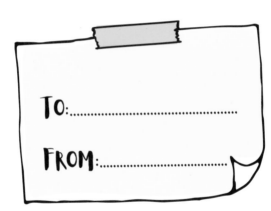

JUST
CHECKING,
YOU DON'T
ACTUALLY
LIKE SLEEP,
DO YOU?

I've conquered a lot of things... knee and foot surgeries... winning grand slams... but I found out by far the hardest is figuring out a stroller!

SERENA WILLIAMS

WHO NEEDS
A SOCIAL LIFE
WHEN YOU CAN
SPEND YOUR
TIME BECOMING
AN EXPERT ON
THE COLOURS
OF BABY POO?

• WELCOME TO PARENTHOOD •

**YOUR HEART
NOW LIVES
INSIDE A SMALL,
UNPREDICTABLE
INSOMNIAC.**

Having children is like
living in a frat house –
nobody sleeps, everything's
broken and there's a
lot of throwing up.

RAY ROMANO

BABY: 1
BABY MANUAL: 0

TOP TIP

Don't fall into the competitive parenting trap. Everybody has good and bad days, whether they admit it or not.

GOING TO THE
TOILET ALONE,
WITH THE DOOR
CLOSED, IS YOUR
NEW SPA DAY.

––––––––––––––––

AH, BABIES!
THEY'RE MORE
THAN JUST
ADORABLE LITTLE
CREATURES ON
WHOM YOU
CAN BLAME
YOUR FARTS.

TINA FEY

NOW IT'S YOUR
TURN TO LIE TO
POTENTIAL NEW
MEMBERS OF THE
BABY CLUB ABOUT
HOW EASY IT ALL IS.

Stop swaying. You already put the baby down.

LEAVING THE HOUSE IS NOW AN EXTREME SPORT.

Suddenly you're
the guy who's floating
in constant jetlag with
an IV of caffeine.

EDDIE REDMAYNE

JUST THINK,
IN A COUPLE
OF YEARS THAT
LITTLE ANGEL
WILL BE CALLING
YOU A POO-HEAD.

• WELCOME TO PARENTHOOD •

**THE COFFEE MAY
HAVE GONE COLD
BUT THE BOSS
IS SUPER-CUTE.**

If we were ever under attack, I would use my wife as a human shield to protect that baby.

RYAN REYNOLDS

TOP TIP

Everybody will want
to give you advice and it
can all seem overwhelming.
Get good at nodding,
changing the subject
and then doing what
you feel is right.

ALL YOU NEED
IS LOVE.
AND BY LOVE
I MEAN BABY
WIPES, WINE
AND A SLEEP.

_____

SLEEP AT THIS
POINT IS JUST
A CONCEPT.
SOMETHING
I'M LOOKING
FORWARD TO
INVESTIGATING
IN THE FUTURE.

AMY POEHLER

· WELCOME TO PARENTHOOD ·

**OTHERWISE
KNOWN AS THE
SLOW DESCENT
INTO BECOMING
YOUR PARENTS.**

You've created a human alarm-clock without a snooze button.

HOW CAN
SOMETHING
SO CUTE BE
SO DIFFICULT
TO DRESS?

Let me give you some baby advice: you're not going to do anything for the next six months.

CHANNING TATUM

IT'S A NEW
STYLE OF
INTERPRETIVE
DANCE WE LIKE
TO CALL BOPPING
AND BOUNCING
(THE BABY
TO SLEEP).

• WELCOME TO PARENTHOOD •

**YOU'RE IN LOVE
WITH A CREATURE
WHO VOMITS
ON YOU.**

Wrinkles are hereditary
– parents get them
from their children.

DORIS DAY

"Sleep when the baby sleeps" is a cliché because it's true. You don't need a tidy house or a Michelin-starred meal to function. Lower your standards.

PLUS-SIDE:
YOU CAN USE
THE PARENTING
PARKING SPACE.
DOWN-SIDE:
YOUR CAR NOW
SMELLS LIKE A
SEWAGE PLANT.

**PARENTING TIP:
IF YOUR CHILD IS
CRYING, HOLD
IT CLOSE AND
WHISPER, "YOU
DON'T HAVE
A CLUE WHAT
HORRORS THIS
WORLD HOLDS."**

ROB DELANEY

> · WELCOME TO PARENTHOOD ·

YOU WILL GROW
TO HATE THE OLD
YOU, BEFORE KIDS,
WHO THOUGHT
THEY KNEW WHAT
TIRED WAS.

Your
baby's
bowel
movements
are your
new
obsession.

TIME HAS
LOST ALL
MEANING;
WE ONLY
DEAL IN
NAPS.

Motherhood is basically finding activities for children in three-hour pockets of time for the rest of your life.

MINDY KALING

NO,
YOUR BABY
PROBABLY ISN'T
COMMUNICATING
WITH YOU VIA
GURGLES.

· WELCOME TO PARENTHOOD ·

**YOUR T-SHIRT IS
ON BACK TO FRONT
AND INSIDE OUT.**

Raising kids is
a walk in the park.
Jurassic Park, that is.

ANONYMOUS

Teething, sleepless nights and development leaps might feel like they last forever, but everything is just a phase. It will pass.

WE ARE ALL JUST
PEOPLE ASKING
OTHER PEOPLE WHAT
"LAY YOUR BABY
DOWN TIRED BUT
NOT OVERTIRED"
ACTUALLY MEANS.

_____

I'VE NEVER HAD
MORE POOP ON
MY PERSON.

JUSTIN TIMBERLAKE

YOUR PHONE IS IN THE FRIDGE AND YOUR PERSONAL HYGIENE IS IN THE BIN.

Don't
open your
mouth
when
changing
a boy.

WIPING UP ALL
THE STAINS
LIKE A
GIANT HUMAN
DISHCLOTH.

A baby changes your
dinner-party conversation
from politics to poops.

MAURICE JOHNSTON

TAKE A
MOMENT TO
APPRECIATE
THE IRONY IN
THE SAYING
"SLEEPING LIKE
A BABY".

· WELCOME TO PARENTHOOD ·

YOUR BABY LOVES YOU SO MUCH THEY WANT TO SAY HELLO TO YOU AT 1 A.M... AND AT 2 A.M... AND 2.30 A.M... AND...

No other stranger cares that your kids ate an artichoke, but you think it's the best story ever.

JIMMY FALLON

Despite all the
boundaries you set,
sometimes you are
going to have to let
the baby win.

NO ONE KNOWS
FRUSTRATION LIKE
A PARENT STUCK
UNDER A NAPPING
BABY UNABLE TO
REACH THE REMOTE.

HAVING AN INFANT
SON ALERTS ME
TO THE FACT THAT
EVERY MAN,
AT ONE POINT,
HAS PEED ON
HIS OWN FACE.

OLIVIA WILDE

· WELCOME TO PARENTHOOD ·

**YOUR BIGGEST DAILY
ACHIEVEMENT
IS NOW GETTING
ANOTHER HUMAN
TO BURP.**

Baby toys are redundant. You are the toy.

HOW CAN
SOMETHING
SO CUTE
SMELL
SO BAD?

When my daughter
is awake I want her to
sleep. When she's asleep
I want her awake. This
is my parenting life.

CHRISSY TEIGEN

I DON'T
WANT TO
SCARE YOU
BUT I THINK
THIS MEANS
YOU'RE A
GROWN-UP.

YOUR NEW NIGHTCLUB DANCE FLOOR IS THE FROZEN AISLE SECTION.

A toy Tamagotchi is
more communicative
than a human baby, OK?
Because a toy will at least
tell you when it poos.

ALI WONG

Keep hold of your
sense of humour.
If you can laugh about
it now, it will stop you
crying about it later.

YOU KNOW
EVERY WORD
TO A DOZEN
NURSERY
RHYMES BUT
HAVE NO IDEA
WHAT DAY IT IS.

_____

I JUST WAKE UP HOPING THAT I DON'T SCREW UP TODAY.

JOHN KRASINSKI

> • WELCOME TO PARENTHOOD •

**YOU WILL CLEAN POO
FROM PLACES YOU
NEVER IMAGINED.**

Sick
stains
are
the
new
black.

100%
POWERED BY
SUGAR AND
COFFEE.

Becoming a mom to me means you have accepted that for the next 16 years of your life, you will have a sticky purse.

NIA VARDALOS

I KNOW WHAT
YOU'RE THINKING
AND NO, I DON'T
KNOW WHY THEY
PUT POCKETS ON
BABY CLOTHES.

**EATING FOOD
WHILE IT'S WARM
ISN'T A THING HERE.**

My new roommate
poops her pants and
doesn't pay rent.

KRISTEN BELL

If you're worried about
being a good parent,
then you probably
already are one.

IT'S NOT THAT
YOU'RE TIRED –
IT'S JUST THAT
YOU TRIED TO
PUT THE BABY'S
SOCKS ON.

A BABY IS AN
INESTIMABLE
BLESSING
AND BOTHER.

MARK TWAIN

I HOPE YOU
PRACTISED
ORIGAMI,
BECAUSE
SWADDLING
IS HARD.

Buttoning up the baby: what fresh hell is this?

THIS HAD
BETTER BE
WORTH IT!

Getting a burp out of your little thing is probably the greatest satisfaction I have come across.

BRAD PITT

YOU DID A
FUNNY THING
THAT MADE YOUR
BABY SMILE!
NOW DO THAT
THING ON
REPEAT UNTIL
YOU HATE IT.

YOUR NEW SAFE
WORD IS "TEETHING";
IT'LL GET YOU OUT
OF ANYTHING.

Even when freshly
washed and relieved of
all obvious confections,
children tend to be sticky.

FRAN LEBOWITZ

Don't put pressure on yourself for things to return to normal. When you start a family you start a whole new normal, so give yourself time to get used to what that is.

TRY TO STOP
ASKING PEOPLE
IF THEY WANT
TO SNIFF YOUR
BABY'S HEAD.

_____

YOU CAN LEARN
MANY THINGS
FROM CHILDREN.
HOW MUCH
PATIENCE YOU
HAVE, FOR
INSTANCE.

FRANKLIN P. JONES

NEW PARENT
CHECKLIST

☑ CO-SLEEPING

☑ CO-EATING

☑ CO-EVERYTHING
WITH YOUR NEW
FAVOURITE PERSON

› • WELCOME TO PARENTHOOD • ‹

BEFORE YOU ASK, YES, THIS IS WHAT YOU SIGNED UP FOR AND NO, THEY DON'T ISSUE REFUNDS.

Your child already has better clothes than you.

PARENTING
WAS SO MUCH
EASIER WHEN
YOU DIDN'T
HAVE KIDS.

I've learned that it's way harder to be a baby... For instance, I haven't thrown up since the nineties and she's thrown up twice since we started this interview.

EVA MENDES

A SWAT TEAM
HAS NOTHING
ON A PARENT
PLANNING
HOW TO GET
THEIR BABY
TO SLEEP.

• WELCOME TO PARENTHOOD •

YOU NOW COMPLAIN ABOUT PEOPLE DOING THE THINGS THAT YOU USED TO LOVE DOING, LIKE HOSTING NOISY HOUSE PARTIES.

I hate when new parents ask who the baby looks like. It was born 15 minutes ago – it looks like a potato.

KEVIN HART

BABY: 1

LAUNDRY PILE: 0

TOP TIP

Now is not the time to
take on new projects,
hobbies or challenges.
Let yourself enjoy the
newborn phase – it'll be
gone before you know it.

YES, THAT'S MY
BABY'S NAME.
NO, I'M NOT GOING
TO CHANGE IT
BECAUSE YOU THINK
"AMELIA" WOULD
SUIT HER BETTER.

24/7.
ONCE YOU SIGN ON
TO BE A MOTHER,
THAT'S THE ONLY
SHIFT THEY OFFER.

JODY PICOULT

**OUR VERSION
OF ROMANCE IS
TAKING YOUR
PARTNER'S TURN TO
CHANGE THE BABY.**

Why does something so small need so much stuff?

YOUR EYES
ARE NOW
EXCLUSIVELY
FOR POKING.

Sometimes going to bed
feels like the highlight
of my day. Ironically,
to my children, bedtime
is a punishment that
violates their basic rights
as human beings.

JIM GAFFIGAN

SINGING
YOUR BABY A
PUNK-ROCK SONG
INSTEAD OF A
LULLABY BECAUSE
YOU ARE A REBEL
LIKE THAT.

> · WELCOME TO PARENTHOOD ·

**WHERE WE GAIN
IMMUNITY BOOSTER
SHOTS FROM VISITS
TO THE SOFT-PLAY
BALL-PIT.**

When my kids become wild
and unruly, I use a nice,
safe playpen. When they're
finished I climb out.

ERMA BOMBECK

Get good at finding small
wins, whether it's half
an hour watching your
favourite show, a bath
while the baby is napping
or making a special lunch.
Build in rewards for
yourself – you deserve it!

PRACTISE BACKING
OUT OF A ROOM
QUICKLY AS SOON
AS YOU SENSE THE
BEGINNING OF THE
BREAST vs BOTTLE
ARGUMENT.

_____

THE FIRST FEW
MONTHS IT WAS
LIKE I TOOK AN
APHRODISIAC.
I WAS TOTALLY
IN LOVE AND
HAD THIS HIGH.

LUCY LIU

PLEASE SAY GOODBYE TO PERSONAL GROOMING.

Trust me, don't open your mouth while bouncing a baby.

FEED,
SLEEP,
CHANGE,
REPEAT.

The quickest way for a
parent to get a child's
attention is to sit down
and look comfortable.

LANE OLINGHOUSE

THE NEW
WALK OF SHAME
IS PUSHING THE
BUGGY AROUND
THE BLOCK AT
3 A.M. TO GET THE
BABY TO SLEEP.

· WELCOME TO PARENTHOOD ·

WHERE POPPING TO THE SHOP FOR MILK, ALONE, QUALIFIES AS AN EXCITING TRIP OUT.

I don't have time for
anything – I'm amazed
I remembered pants!

RYAN REYNOLDS

You are raising a small human, not a robot. You and your baby will have very different ideas about how you want to do things — it'll take a ~~little~~ lot of compromise from both of you.

DON'T
BELIEVE THEM:
IT'S NOT GAS,
IT'S A SMILE.

IT'S SO FUNNY
BECAUSE THEY'RE
NOT STRONG
ENOUGH TO KILL
YOU. AND THEY
WANT TO KILL
YOU SO BAD!
THEY CAN'T KILL
YOU. NOT YET.
TRY AGAIN IN A
COUPLE YEARS.

TINA FEY

YOU ARE GOING TO DO SOME VERY RANDOM INTERNET SEARCHES.

No,
MENSA
doesn't
accept
applications
for babies.

YOU'RE
GOING
TO NEED
MORE
COFFEE.

Having a new baby
is like suddenly
getting the world's
worst roommate.

ANNE LAMOTT

THE ONLY THING
STANDING IN
THE WAY OF
YOU BEING A
PERFECT PARENT
IS YOUR CHILD.

> **· WELCOME TO PARENTHOOD ·**

**PROBABLY BEST
NOT TO LOOK
IN THE MIRROR
TOO CLOSELY
FOR A WHILE.**

They tell you that at his
age all they do is eat,
sleep and poop. And what
I've learned is they can
actually do all three at the
same time. Who knew?

JOSH DUHAMEL

BABY: 1
CONCEPT OF TIME: 0

TOP TIP

Baby blues are normal, but if yours don't seem to be lifting then speak to your doctor. The biggest gift you can give your baby is taking care of yourself.

THE TEETHING
TOY IS NOT A
TEETHING TOY.
YOU ARE THE
TEETHING TOY.
_____

I WANT MY CHILDREN TO HAVE ALL THE THINGS I COULDN'T AFFORD. THEN I WANT TO MOVE IN WITH THEM.

PHYLLIS DILLER

> **· WELCOME TO PARENTHOOD ·**

DO NOT ENTER IF YOU ARE SENSITIVE TO SOUND, SLEEP DEPRIVATION OR BAD SMELLS.

Goodbye
lazy
Sundays
(or lazy
any days).

BINGE-WATCHING
YOUR BABY
LIKE IT'S THE
BEST SHOW
EVER.

Sleep? Yes, I have a
vague recollection of
what that was like.

ANONYMOUS

IT'S A SHAME
YOU AREN'T A
PARENTING EXPERT
LIKE EVERY
SINGLE STRANGER
YOU AND YOUR
BABY MEET.

⟩ • WELCOME TO PARENTHOOD • ⟨

**WHERE YOU'LL
DISCOVER THE
BIZARRE FEELING
OF WANTING TO
BE AWAY FROM
SOMEONE AND
MISSING THEM AT
THE SAME TIME.**

He's looking for
danger at all times.
We're just trying to
keep him alive.

JASON SUDEIKIS ON HIS SON

TOP TIP

Get comfortable with accepting help from friends and family and practise asking for it. You don't get a medal for being a martyr and doing it all on your own.

PACKING FOR A
TRIP TO THE PARK
LIKE IT'S A TWO-
WEEK HOLIDAY
TO MEXICO.

WHY DON'T KIDS UNDERSTAND THAT THEIR NAP IS NOT FOR THEM BUT FOR US?

ALYSON HANNIGAN

**THE DAYS ARE LONG
AND THE NIGHTS
ARE EVEN LONGER.**

Look how
cute my
cute my
baby is.
NO, LOOK!

If you're interested in finding out more about our books, find us on Facebook at **Summersdale Publishers**, on Twitter at **@Summersdale** and on Instagram at **@summersdalebooks** and get in touch. We'd love to hear from you!

www.summersdale.com